PURPOSE IS A DECISION

DISCOVER, DEVELOP AND DISSEMINATE
THE RICHES WITHIN YOU

Purpose is a Decision:
Discover, Develop and Disseminate the Riches within You

RR Creative Press
Dallas, TX

The publisher is not responsible for the websites (or their content) that are not owned by the publisher.

Printed in the United States of America
First edition: March 2012

DEDICATION

Purpose is a Decision is dedicated to:
my parents for their great support over the years
and to my Aunt Portia for her priceless investment of time,
affection and love which she planted in me.
Aunt Portia lived from 1941-2012. I send her off in joy;
I lead her out in peace. The mountains and the hills
shout into singing; the trees of the field applaud
with clapping for a life well lived.

CONTENTS

ACKNOWLEDGEMENTS

Much appreciation to my wife who eloquently supports me in fulfilling the mission God has granted to me.

Sincere gratitude for the faithful leadership and tutelage of Dr. Tony Evans for modeling what it looks like to be a Kingdom-minded man.

A heartfelt thank you to Bobby Gibson for his Barnabus spirit to see the best in people, his humility and for always leading by example.

Words can't express how appreciative I am to Ruth Reed, my editor and designer. She is simply…gifted, creative and brilliant.

Introduction

Most of us want to achieve and reach our full potential in life. We want to experience God's best. We desire to obtain our divine purpose. Yet, most people go to their grave with their best stuff still in them. We go to our grave with books unwritten, songs unheard, music unwritten, poetry unspoken, love unshared and businesses uncreated.

What I have observed from God's Word and life is that there is a cycle to obtaining one's purpose...regardless of race, age, gender, social or financial status or who you know or don't know. One cannot walk into your purpose without facing your giant. In other words, the road to success, the road to achievement, or better yet, the path to your dream must cross through the River of Fear — whether it is the fear of failure, the fear of success, the fear of hard work, the fear of the unknown or the fear of obstacles.

It is my firm belief that adversity is the gatekeeper to success. Success is defined as that ability to carry out the divine design and resources God has placed within you at birth. It is the fulfillment of purpose. It has nothing to do with money, position or status per se. True success is carrying out your purpose, and your purpose is something only God has created you to fulfill.

Adversity appears, at first, as opposition to your ability to experience success. However, it often becomes an instrument for your good that can guide you down a path that you would not have likely traveled on your own. When you travel through this valley of adversity, it often reveals to you a valuable tool that enhances your ability to see your purpose fulfilled. The mindset of the successful is that every adversity has within it the equivalent seed of opportunity.

God has said, that He has already created good works for you and I to carry out. The children of Israel were supposed to possess the Promised Land in Canaan, yet their lack of faith—the inability to believe what the human eye could not conceive—prevented them from fulfilling their purpose at that time in their cycle. Lack of faith will always prevent you from possessing your Promised Land. What God has prepared and put within you to carry out is often unfulfilled until you have the courage to put feet to your faith—for faith is the launch pad to your success.

Do you realize that God prepared all your gifts and talents uniquely for you on the day you were created? Your gifts and talents are precious and priceless. In fact, there is a wealth of resources deposited within you since the beginning of time—before you even existed.

"You were in Eden, the garden of God; Every precious stone was your covering; The sardius, topaz, and diamond, Berly, onyx, and jasper, Sapphire, turquoise, and emerald with gold. The workmanship of your timbrels and pipes was prepared for you on the day you were created." (Ezekiel 28:13)

Your greatest resources—an unlimited wealth of resources—are within you! There is rich stuff on the inside of you, just waiting to be realized. It is my prayer that you ask, not for more external things, but for more wisdom to use what God has internally placed within you when you were created. When you discover these riches and develop the resources within, then you are ready to disseminate the resources.

Dissemination of the resources within is equivalent to sowing seeds. Once you have sown and given away what God has so graciously put within you, then your purpose takes on a mindset of its own. I call this "the Law of Multiplication." This law works like this: the resources within you act like a seed—when planted, they always produce more.

This is the goal. This is the divine design—to duplicate and demonstrate our Savior's model of giving and spreading love. There is no better or more effective way to spread love then to share and give away the resources God has divinely put within you. Will you join the forces of that small population to discover, develop and disseminate the riches within you? Purpose is a decision. So if you're ready, let's begin now!

The Cycle of a Purpose Fulfilled

*"There is one quality which one must possess to win,
and that is definiteness of purpose, the knowledge
of what one wants, and a burning desire to possess it."
-Napoleon Hill*

T here are eight stages that you will go through to experience your purpose fulfilled. Let me explain the eight stages of the cycle of a purpose fulfilled.

STAGE 1: Your Purpose is Predestined: God's Divine Design

"Your eyes saw me when I was inside the womb. All the days ordained for me were recorded in your scroll before one of them came into existence." (Psalms 139:16 NET)

"For we are his workmanship, having been created in Christ Jesus for good works that God prepared beforehand so we may do them." (Ephesians 2:10 NET)

'God said, "Let the land produce vegetation: plants yielding seeds according to their kinds, and trees bearing fruit with seed in it according to their kinds." It was so.' (Genesis 1:11 NET)

If God created the fruit and vegetation with seed already in it, surely you and I have seeds within us. Each of these passages underscore a very important point — we all possess talents, gifts, abilities and ideas that God has entrusted to us and deposited within us. Sadly, most people go to their graves with their best stuff still inside them. Determine you will not diminish or discount the purpose you were created for.

Once you understand your purpose is predestined, then you're ready for the next stage.

Stage 2: Your Purpose is Aroused.
Before this stage, you are unaware of your purpose and the seeds of talent within you. This is a time of awakening and a growing awareness of the gifts and abilities God has put within you. This is a time of great excitement and anticipation of what you can become as your eyes are opened, and you begin to discover the riches, wealth and resources that God has placed in you at birth.

Stage 3: Your Purpose is Envisioned.
This is a time of dreaming — a time of creating a mental picture of what your life will look like once you reach your destination. During this stage you envision the possibility of what your life can become. This is the stage of imagination. This stage is vital and can yield unimaginable possibilities for you. Do you realize that everything that exists today first began with an idea? Henry Ford's V-8 Model T started with an idea. Steve Jobs started with an idea to create a keyless computer, but in the process, the idea to create a phone like no other was birthed. As a result, we have the iPhone® today.

Stage 4: Your Purpose is Pursued.
This is a time of great action! This is when you need to take the vi-

THE CYCLE OF A PURPOSE FULFILLED

sion and mission you have and put feet to it. It is a time of doing. However, one must be careful that as you pursue the mission, you do not forsake the Master of the mission. As you put feet to your vision, things may start going well, and life can be very good. It can be very exciting to see parts of your purpose unfold, and your vision begin to manifest, but stage five is coming.

Stage 5: Your Purpose is Blocked.
Out of nowhere, it seems as though every-thing dries up. The flow has reached a dam. This is a time of great challenge. It's a time of disappointment and discour-agement — a time of frustration and fear. It can be a time of kicking and screaming for you, because what has been envisioned, no longer seems possible. This is a time of spiritual temper tantrums. It is important that you recognize what is going on at this phase and stage. This is a time of spiritual growth and personal development.

"A blocked path also offers guidance."
-Mason Cooley

Our development personally and spiritually is much like the natural development of a child. When you were born, you came out of your mother's womb totally dependent. You could do nothing for yourself. They fed you. They carried you. They even cleaned up after you. Then you started to crawl, walk and gradually became less dependent and more independent. Eventually, you had to grow up and take re-sponsibility for your own personal growth. As you grew, life got more challenging and more complex than the simple ex-istence you had as a baby. The same is true of your purpose.

You may experience the excitement of birthing a new purpose and be initially overjoyed with the beginning baby steps of your dream coming to pass. But as your purpose grows and develops, so does the responsibility and challenges you face. You begin to face challenges you never thought you would encounter. The obstacles seem bigger than you could have imagined. This is the stage when you come face-to-face with your River of Fear! It is here that you have to make one of three life-changing and purpose-defining decisions:

1. Cross through it
When the children of Israel crossed though the Red Sea, it had to be a scary day. They had never seen anyone walk through a sea before; I am sure. They had no sail boat, no scuba gear and no snorkeling equipment. Perhaps they would have never crossed it, had the Egyptians not been chasing after them. Always remember, every adversity has the equivalent seed of opportunity within it, so choose to cross your river.

2. Get comfortable at the river
In Genesis 11 Terah, Abram's father, has the intention and vision to relocate his family to Canaan. However, verses 31-32 says that he settled in Haran. He never crossed his river. He became comfortable, stuck and complacent and never saw his purpose fulfilled. Don't make the mistake of settling in and getting stuck at your River of Fear.

3. Cuss at it
It is here that you must be careful—when you begin to cuss, fuss and complain. This is a slippery slope for dissatisfaction and leads to discontent-ment, which leads to discouragement. This phase is vitally important. How you respond will determine if you ever reach

"Dissatisfaction leads to discontent-ment. Discontentment leads to discouragement. Discouragement leads to despair."
-Guy E. Earle

your destination. If you cuss at your river when faced with opposition and allow your strength to wane, you will despise your purpose.

Esau was a man who despised his purpose. Esau and his descendants were lusty, passionate and profane people who lived for the moment. Genesis 25:24 says, "Esau despised his birthright." Esau was ungrateful for his birthright. He undervalued it, and he did not see its worth until it was no longer in his possession. Many may think that he had no choice since he was going to die if he didn't eat. Upon first reading the passage in Genesis, it would appear to be so; however, the New Testament expounds on the nature and character of Esau and his descendants. They lived for the moment, and they had a spirit of impatience and instant gratification. Esau was hungry, but I seriously doubt he was going to die. He wanted what he wanted, and he wanted it now.

You must learn to value the riches and resources within you. See its worth and appreciate it — for you can put no price tag on it. Its value is worth millions or even billions of dollars if you learn to discover, develop and disseminate it.

Another who failed to appreciate his gift and seed was Onan.

"But Onan knew that the child would not be considered his so whenever he had sexual relations with his brother's wife, he withdrew premature so as not to give his brother a descendent...what he did was evil in the Lord's sight so the Lord killed him." (Genesis 38:9-10)

Onan's selfish act was all about not wanting to give his seed to be a blessing to his brothers descendents. You must understand this important principle: when you only use the riches within you for you, you can never experience the "law of multiplication." It is in giving, that one experiences true joy!

Accomplishing your dream and seeing your purpose come to fruition is a matter of the heart. You can overcome adversities, no matter how big they are. As the saying goes, "It is not the size of the dog in the fight, but the fight inside the dog." Proverbs 24:10 states it this way, "If you faint in the day of trouble, your strength is small." You can get to the next stage in the cycle of a purpose ful-

> "Adversity has the effect of eliciting talents, which in prosperous circumstances would have lain dormant."
> -Horace

filled, if you understand what Paul said, "Don't grow weary in well doing, for you shall reap if you faint not." (Galatians 6:9-10)

Stage 6: Your Purpose is Put on Hold.
This stage is a time of spiritual renewal—a time of refreshing and a time of replenishing and reviving. You have just come off a time of breaking and a time of battle, and you need to rest. This is the phase of waiting. This stage can be frustrating unless you remember that after you have done all you can, you have to know that it is God that ultimately completes what He has begun in you. This concept can be paradoxical because on one hand you have to act and walk in faith, yet on the other hand you have to depend on God.

Psalms 23:3 says in part, "He restores my strength..." This is a time of refueling. When you come out of having your purpose put on hold, you come out renewed and refreshed. Your second wind has kicked in.

Stage 7: Your Purpose is Resurrected.

Stage seven is a time of revision—a time to change some things. This is your time to leave old habits behind. It is a time of refocusing to make sure that when you get to your promised land, you keep first things first.

"But seek first the kingdom of God and His righteousness, and all these things shall be added to you." (Matthew 6:33)

As your purpose is resurrected, it's time to face your River of Fear again. As you do, remember God's presence, protection, provision and power! It's a time to remember 1 John 4:17-18 which says in part, "Perfect love casts out fear..." That perfect "passion" or intensity casts out fear.

Stage seven is when God rings the bell and says, "it is time to do battle again." This is a time of action, but often it is revised actions and more dependence on the power of God than before you got to this stage. When you face your River of Fear this time, you are challenged with the three C's again. You can cross it, get comfortable at the banks of the River, or you can cuss at it.

When Israel was doing battle against the Philistines, they came face-to-face with the giant Goliath. They were all afraid and unwilling to face their fear. Yet, there was one who had courage, ability and faith in God. David comprehended the resources God had already put within him and the reassurance that God would be with him. He, like very few people, experienced his purpose fulfilled, because he faced the giant of fear. It is when you face adversity that adversity surrenders to you the keys to the door called success. Which leads us to stage eight.

Remember God's ① Presence ② Protection ③ Provision ④ Power

① Comprehend the resources of God
② Reassurances that God will be with me
Courage ability faith in God

Stage 8: Your Purpose is Experienced.

Once you cross the River of Fear by faith, your purpose is experienced and realized, because it is now harvest time! Throughout the Bible, God shows us that there is a seed time and harvest time. There is a time of sowing and reaping. Yet, it is very important that you not get too comfortable. Just as quick as you get to the top, you can get knocked back down, if you loose focus. You must know that when you arrive at your promised land, you are not home free. Your purpose and dream is not a one-stop place, but a matter of continuation.

Once you arrive at your destination, you must not forget the lessons you learned on the path and journey to your purpose fulfilled. As you experience the joy of reaping, realize and relish in the fact that reaping is fulfilled only because sowing preceded it. So as you reap, simultaneously sow.

If you ever built a fire, you know it takes wood and a lighter to ignite the flames. Even though the fire is kindled, it will burn out, if you don't continue to rekindle it with wood. If you fail to rekindle it, you will not experience warmth in the midst of cold temperatures. So it is with the riches and resources within you. If you don't continue to unleash and disseminate the wealth bestowed upon you from God, you will not continue to experience the law of multiplication. It is like having a 401k in which your company will match up to five percent of what you invest in yourself. This, for the financial savvy, is a no-brainer. It is a way to double your money for free. When you sow what God has put within you, he multiples it beyond your mental capacities of comprehension.

Now that you are familiar with the eight stages of a purpose fulfilled, let's take a look at the big picture again. I have come

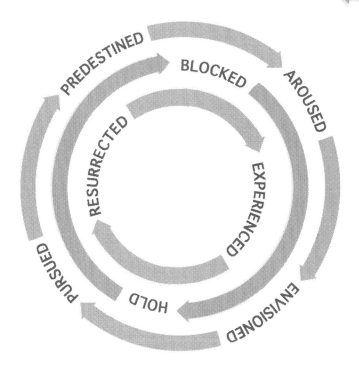

up with this illustration to show you that at any point in your life you can find yourself at any stage of a purpose fulfilled. In fact, you might be pursuing your purpose as it relates to your finances and experiencing overflow but feel on hold in another area of your purpose. It's a cycle, and you will experience God moving you from level to level throughout different seasons of your life. The purpose cycle will last your whole life long. In fact, just as you sense yourself reaching the fulfillment of your dream, God will place a new and bigger dream on the inside of you. He doesn't want you growing stagnant, and He always has more people in mind that He wants you to be a blessing to.

If you stick with God's principles and processes you will see your purpose fulfilled and experience harvest in your life and countless others.

Let's continue on our journey and take a look at how this cycle unfolded in the lives of those who have gone before us and see what we can learn from their cycle of a purpose fulfilled.

CHAPTER
TWO

Israel's Cycle from Victim to Victor

"It is impossible to win the race unless you venture to run,
impossible to win the victory unless you dare to battle."
-Richard M. Devos

T he next few chapters will illustrate the cycle of a purpose fulfilled, as described in chapter one, using the children of Israel, king David, Jesus and Walt Disney.

1. Israel's Purpose is Predestined.

"Abram passed through the land to the place of Shechem, as far as the terebinth tree of Moreh. And the Canaanites were then in the land. Then the Lord appeared to Abram and said, 'To your descendants I will give this land.' " (Genesis 12:6-7)

God told Abram I have a plan for you, and that plan is to increase your descendants as numerous as the stars and give them the land of Canaan. Abram was not successful, just a regular man and was most likely struck with shock and amazement with such a lofty and lavish promise. Most likely, he didn't see it as possible in the natural.

2. Israel's Purpose is Aroused.
In the book of Numbers in chapter 33, the journey of Israel is reviewed. After Joseph brings the children of Israel to Egypt, they have become so enormous that the Egyptians make them

PURPOSE IS A DECISION

slaves. God raises up Moses to deliver the people from Pharaoh. Then verse 3 says, "They departed from Ramses in the first month, on the fifteenth day of the first month; on the day after the Passover the children of Israel went out with boldness in the sight of all the Egyptians."

The Children of Israel experienced severe hardship and slavery under an iron hand along with great emotional abuse. Yet, they went out in boldness from the Egyptians. They saw the possibility of a purpose fulfilled. They, who once only saw hardship, failure and no end from the hand of the Egyptians, now had a renewed faith of what they could become. In their mind, they were most likely thinking, "just maybe what was promised can become a reality."

Leaving with boldness was an expression of the Israelites' confidence, excitement and arousal. They were eager to carry on to see what else God had in store.

3. Israel's Purpose is Envisioned.
As they were exiting, the Israelites began to envision what could happen—that perhaps the prophesy was correct, and they would become a great nation.

After the children of Israel crossed the Red Sea, they sang this song of praise:

"I will sing to the Lord, For He has triumphed gloriously!
The horse and its rider
He has thrown into the sea!
The Lord is my strength and song,
And He has become my salvation;
He is my God, and I will praise Him;

My father's God, and I will exalt Him.
The Lord is a man of war;
The Lord is His name."
(Exodus 15:1-3)

"If you can believe, all things are possible."
-Mark 9:23

This is a vivid picture of the confidence they had in God. They had previously heard about God, but now they had experienced the power of God firsthand. It was a moment of them acknowledging, "I am a believer now. I can see clearly now that the rain is gone!"

4. Israel's Purpose is Pursued.

"And the Lord went before them by day in a pillar of cloud to lead the way, and by night in a pillar of fire to give them light, so as to go by day and night." (Exodus 13:21)

This was a time of great action. Israel was covered as they moved forward with a cloud by day and fire by night. They experienced God's provision in several ways: bitter waters were turned sweet and they received manna from Heaven along with all-you-can-eat quail. In Exodus 17, it speaks of how God helped them defeat the Amalekites. They also received the Ten Commandments, and the Levites were given rituals on how to maintain a right relationship with God. They were cruising, victory after victory, miracle after miracle and blessing after blessing. Life was good, but adversity was coming.

5. Israel's Purpose is Blocked.
Numbers 13 and Deuteronomy 1:19-21 recounts how Israel's purpose became blocked.

'So we departed from Horeb, and went through all that great and terrible wilderness which you saw on the way to the mountains of the Amorites, as the Lord our God had commanded us. Then we came to Kadesh Barnea. And I said to you, "You have come to the mountains of the Amorites, which the Lord our God is giving us. Look, the Lord your God has set the land before you; go up and possess it, as the Lord God of your fathers has spoken to you; do not fear or be discouraged."' (Deuteronomy 1:19-21)

Despite God's promise, Numbers 14:22-31 reveals how Israel despised their purpose and promise. Verse 31 says in part, "and they shall know the land you have despised."

The children of Israel had seen the hand of God, victory after victory, miracle after miracle, and blessing after blessing. Yet, when they saw and heard about the land of Canaan, they believed it was too good for them to possess. They believed they didn't deserve it, and they weren't strong enough or big enough to do what God had predestined.

You must always know that what God has predestined for you to do is never too big and never impossible. It is not about your ability or your capability. It is about your capacity to believe that what God intends, He can accomplish. It appeared that the children of Israel had the capacity to believe, but like most people, when they come face-to-face with the River of Fear or a giant problem, they find out how small their perspective of God really is. It is a great reminder that accomplishing purpose is more about God's

"We ask ourselves 'who am I to be brilliant, gorgeous, talented and fabulous?' Actually, who are you not to be? You are a child of God."
-Marianne Williamson

ability and your availability and less about your ability and capability.

6. Israel's Purpose is Put on Hold.
In Numbers 14:34, the Israelites are sentenced by God to wander for 40 years. Despite their purpose being delayed, God was still faithful.

"And I have led you forty years in the wilderness. Your clothes have not worn on you, and your sandals have not worn out on your feet." (Deuteronomy 29:5)

There are normally three reasons God will set you in a holding pattern:
1. Punishment
2. Preparation
3. Protection

Punishment
The children of Israel were put into "time out." They had disobeyed God, and God disciplined them for their disobedience. Punishment is not mere exercise of one's authority. The ultimate goal of punishment is to change behavior.

Preparation
You, like most people, may want to jump into the battle of the elite and successful immediately. Yet, it is the lessons learned prior to facing one's giant that foster confidence in your God-given ability and in God Almighty.

Protection
One of the greatest lessons you can learn is that delay doesn't equate to failure. Delay is often similar to a person who is

driving and has decided to pull over for a minute to make a call. When they get back on the path headed to their destination, they observe a horrible accident. As they begin to ponder the negative event, they realize that if they hadn't pulled over, they would have been the one in the accident. Delay can be in your best interest. Whether you are in the holding pattern of finding your significant other, landing the perfect job, completing a degree or starting your own business, delay can be one of your greatest assets.

7. Israel's Purpose is Resurrected.

"Hear, O Israel: The Lord our God, the Lord is one! You shall love the Lord your God with all your heart, with all your soul, and with all your strength." (Deuteronomy 6:4-5)

The book of Deuteronomy is a time for the Israelites to remember to keep God first.

It's a time of revision for the Israelites, so they don't make the same mistakes. I like to think of this stage as the pre-game warm-up.

"…the great trials which your eyes have seen, the signs, and those great wonders. Yet the Lord has not given you a heart to perceive and eyes to see and ears to hear, to this very day." (Deuteronomy 29:3-4)

God was telling the Israelites, "I am the one who hindered your understanding and comprehension of what I was doing. I am the one who blinded you, who caused you not to be able to hear the message sent by me. But as of this day, I have opened up your understanding; I have opened your eyes and caused you to be able to hear with clarity what I have been saying." In other words, "God will wake you up when it is time!" In the meantime, go to sleep while in the holding pattern. Your Heavenly Father is at the driving wheel, and He doesn't need your help.

8. Israel's Purpose is Experienced.
Here Israel crosses its River of Fear, but this time, they go into the enemy's territory with the full armor of God. God instructs them when they go in to take up the Ark of the Covenant. Please know this: You cannot expect to defeat anyone if God is not with you and fighting on your behalf. God tells Israel that He will give them victory and success little by little.

"And the Lord your God will drive out those nations before you little by little; you will be unable to destroy them at once, lest the beasts of the field become too numerous for you." (Deuteronomy 7:22)

When God causes you to finally realize your purpose, know that your success will come little by little. Success is not a one stop shop. It is a continuation of successes and victories. As you grow, so does your territory of impact.

The concept of God developing us little by little is seen in the life of David. He went from a shepherd boy to shepherding a nation. However, this process was no overnight success story. This was a tiresome journey of victories, betrayal, heartache and pain — not to mention loneliness.

David's Cycle from Kid to King

"There can be no failure to a man who has not lost his courage, his character, his self respect, or his self-confidence. He is still a King."
-Orison Swett Marden

D avid is probably one of the Bible's greatest success stories, yet his path to purpose has just as many failures and setbacks as successes. David experienced the lowest lows and the greatest disappointments.   However, God fulfilled his purpose plan for David, and He will do the same for you. If David went from a kid to a king, you can know that how you start doesn't have to be how you finish. Your greatest role may still be yet to come, if you let the purpose cycle unfold.

1. David's Purpose is Predestined.

"Now the Lord said to Samuel, "How long will you mourn for Saul, seeing I have rejected him from reigning over Israel? Fill your horn with oil, and go; I am sending you to Jesse the Bethlehemite. For I have provided Myself a king among his sons." (1 Samuel 16:1)

What a vivid picture of God's purpose revealed! Even though God planned for David to be King, David didn't experience the position of King for quite some time.

2. David's Purpose is Aroused.

"So he sent and brought him in. Now he was ruddy, with bright eyes, and good-looking. And the Lord said, "Arise, anoint him; for this is the one!" Then Samuel took the horn of oil and anointed him in the midst of his brothers; and the Spirit of the Lord came upon David from that day forward. So Samuel arose and went to Ramah." (1 Samuel 16:12-13)

David goes on to defeat Goliath further arousing God's purpose in his life. Although David was the least of his brothers in his earthly father's eyes, he was viewed as the favored son from his Heavenly Father's eyes. What a beautiful picture of redemption! After many have written you off and not taken you seriously or just have failed to see the divine potential within you, know that as long as God sees it, that is all that truly matters!

3. David's Purpose is Envisioned.
During this stage of the dream cycle, David began to ponder thinking, "Just maybe, I am fit to be a king, even though my father didn't see my potential and my brothers accused me of being too nosey and up to no good." What happened with the prophet Samuel was just beginning to sink in, and David was beginning to see himself as a king and not a kid!

4. David's Purpose is Pursued.
In 1 Samuel 18:5-7, several things can be learned about how David's purpose unfolded. First, Saul didn't let him go home, but set him over the men of war instead. Second, David experienced victory after victory and success after success. In fact, he was so successful that the women sang a song of praise for all his victories. Life was good for David. He was receiving applauses and great recognition and in his mind, he most likely believed that his appointment to be king would happen very soon. However, stage five was coming, because the door to

success is through adversity. Consider adversity as the gatekeeper to your success.

5. David's Purpose is Blocked.

"Adversity is
the gatekeeper
to success."
-Guy E. Earle

David's purpose wasn't without challenges.

"Then Saul was very angry, and the saying displeased him; and he said, "They have ascribed to David ten thousands, and to me they have ascribed only thousands. Now what more can he have but the kingdom?" So Saul eyed David from that day forward....And Saul cast the spear, for he said, "I will pin David to the wall!" (1 Samuel 18:8-9, 11)

David's path to purpose was literally a life and death experience, but David learned to encourage himself throughout this stage.

Your purpose may be blocked by someone you would never have thought possible. People are unpredictable, and those who appear in your corner the most may just be the mole. Jesus knew his mole, yet he still chose to embrace him because Judas (otherwise known as adversity) was a key factor in setting the stage for his success.

6. David's Purpose is Put on Hold.
1 Samuel 23:14 points out that David stayed in the strongholds in the wilderness. Strongholds were the mountain heights of the wilderness. Although David was anointed to be the next king, his purpose had yet to unfold completely. This was a waiting period for him.

"Now the time that David dwelt in the country of the Philistines was one full year and four months." (1 Samuel 27:7)

7. David's Purpose is Resurrected.
While David was still living amongst the Philistines, God began to resurrect David's purpose.

"And David and his men went up and raided the Geshurites, the Girzites, and the Amalekites. For those nations were the inhabitants of the land from of old, as you go to Shur, even as far as the land of Egypt." (1 Samuel 23:14)

This was a time of pursuing again for David, yet this stage wasn't without its setbacks. While away at battle, the city of Ziklag was raided by the enemy, and David's family, and those of the men with him, were taken captive. David immediately inquired of the Lord what to do. After receiving instructions to pursue, David and his men went up and raided the Geshurites recovering all and taking great treasure from their enemies. With each success, God confirmed He was still with David and would fulfill His plan for David's life. David was getting his courage back after being broken and lonely. He learned through that valley experience that if God is all you have, He is all you will ever need.

"Life is a series of experiences, each one of which makes us bigger, even though sometimes it is hard to realize this. For the world was built to develop character, and we must learn that the setbacks and griefs which we endure help us in our marching onward."
-Henry Ford

8. David's Purpose is Experienced.
In this stage, David begins to experience his purpose, but it still comes little by little. In Samuel 2:4 it reads, "Then the men of Judah came, and there they anointed David king over the house of Judah." Notice the whole kingdom wasn't given to David at once. In this passage, he was made King of Judah. It isn't until later, in 2 Samuel 5:3, that he was anointed king over all of Israel.

Jesus' Cycle from Manager Boy to Majestic King

"There is nothing worth living for, unless it is worth dying for."
-Elizabeth Elliott

Jesus was born in Nazareth, and it was said, "Can any good thing come from Nazareth?" The clash of race, class, and gender has been going on since the beginning of time. You may judge others by their place of birth, or you may be judged by your place of birth. You may judge others by their race, or you may be judged by your race. You may judge others by their neighborhood, or you may be judged by your neighborhood. One thing the examples of a purpose fulfilled show is that what a person can become is not easily detected in the infant or seed state.

In fact, every creation of God has within them a seed that can take on the form of a savior. Yes—upon first hearing this, it appears to be blasphemy, for we are not God, nor can we be God. But we are made in the image of God, and we are to be conforming to the character of God. The Bible says to "have this mind in you, which was also in Christ Jesus." (Philippians 2:5) According to www.dictionary.com, the word savior is defined as, "A person who saves, rescues, or delivers." The riches God has placed within you have been supplied to make a difference, to save, rescue, deliver or empower others.

One of the men who has greatly impacted and influenced my life is Dr. Tony Evans, Senior Pastor of Oak Cliff Bible Fellowship. He has eloquently said, "You are designed to be a conduit and not a cul-de-sac." A conduit is someone that allows things to flow through them. My plea is that you begin to see yourselves as a little savior. Recognize that God has distributed within you a gift—a treasure that if unleashed and disseminated, will bless you. However, you need to first be a blessing to others. You can only be a little savior when you give the riches and wealth God has placed in you away. Let's examine how the Savior of the world did just that.

> "You are designed to be a conduit and not a cul-de-sac."
> -Dr. Tony Evans

1. Jesus' Purpose is Predestined.
Throughout the Old Testament there are numerous prophecies concerning Jesus' purpose. In Numbers 24:17, Jesus was prophesied about by Balaaim saying, "I see Him, but not now; I behold Him, but not near; A Star shall come out of Jacob; A Scepter shall rise out of Israel..." Genesis 49:10 reads, "The scepter shall not depart from Judah." A scepter is a symbol of kingship. In fact, Jesus was a direct descendent of King David. Matthew records the genealogy of Jesus Christ.

"The book of the genealogy of Jesus Christ, the Son of David, the Son of Abraham: Abraham begot Isaac, Isaac begot Jacob, and Jacob begot Judah and his brothers. Judah begot Perez and Zerah by Tamar, Perez begot Hezron, and Hezron begot Ram. Ram begot Amminadab, Amminadab begot Nahshon, and Nahshon begot Salmon.

Salmon begot Boaz by Rahab, Boaz begot Obed by Ruth, Obed begot Jesse, and Jesse begot David the king.

David the king begot Solomon by her who had been the wife of Uriah. Solomon begot Rehoboam, Rehoboam begot Abijah, and Abijah begot Asa. Asa begot Jehoshaphat, Jehoshaphat begot Joram, and Joram begot Uzziah. Uzziah begot Jotham, Jotham begot Ahaz, and Ahaz begot Hezekiah. Hezekiah begot Manasseh, Manasseh begot Amon, and Amon begot Josiah. Josiah begot Jeconiah and his brothers about the time they were carried away to Babylon.

And after they were brought to Babylon, Jeconiah begot Shealtiel, and Shealtiel begot Zerubbabel. Zerubbabel begot Abiud, Abiud begot Eliakim, and Eliakim begot Azor. Azor begot Zadok, Zadok begot Achim, and Achim begot Eliud. Eliud begot Eleazar, Eleazar begot Matthan, and Matthan begot Jacob. And Jacob begot Joseph the husband of Mary, of whom was born Jesus who is called Christ.

So all the generations from Abraham to David are fourteen generations, from David until the captivity in Babylon are fourteen generations, and from the captivity in Babylon until the Christ are fourteen generations." (Matthew 1:1-16)

Jesus purpose was predestined. The amazing thing is that the genealogy of Jesus is not filled with perfect people. It has people of different races, social and economic classes and all of them were divinely and sovereignly designed to fulfill the prophesy of the Messiah—Jesus the Christ—Savior of mankind.

2. Jesus' Purpose is Aroused
It is important to note that Jesus' purpose was sparked at a young age although it would be many years before He walked in the fullness of it.

"So when they had performed all things according to the law of the Lord, they returned to Galilee, to their own city, Nazareth. And the Child grew and became strong in spirit, filled with wisdom; and the grace of God was upon Him. His parents went to Jerusalem every year at the Feast of the Passover. And when He was twelve years old, they went up to Jerusalem according to the custom of the feast. When they had finished the days, as they returned, the Boy Jesus lingered behind in Jerusalem. And Joseph and His mother did not know it; but supposing Him to have been in the company, they went a day's journey, and sought Him among their relatives and acquaintances. So when they did not find Him, they returned to Jerusalem, seeking Him.

Now so it was that after three days they found Him in the temple, sitting in the midst of the teachers, both listening to them and asking them questions. And all who heard Him were astonished at His understanding and answers. So when they saw Him, they were amazed; and His mother said to Him, "Son, why have You done this to us? Look, Your father and I have sought You anxiously." And He said to them, "Why did you seek Me? Did you not know that I must be about My Father's business?" But they did not understand the statement which He spoke to them.

Then He went down with them and came to Nazareth, and was subject to them, but His mother kept all these things in her heart. And Jesus increased in wisdom and stature, and in favor with God and men." (Luke 2:39-52)

As a young boy of 12, Jesus knew He must be about His Father's business and carry out His purpose. He was created to be a conduit and not a cul-de-sac.

3. Jesus' Purpose is Envisioned
A key event in Jesus' purpose was His baptism by John the Baptist.

'Then Jesus came from Galilee to John at the Jordan to be baptized by him. And John tried to prevent Him, saying, "I need to be baptized by You, and are You coming to me?" But Jesus answered and said to him, "Permit it to be so now, for thus it is fitting for us to fulfill all righteousness." Then he allowed Him. When He had been baptized, Jesus came up immediately from the water; and behold, the heavens were opened to Him, and He saw the Spirit of God descending like a dove and alighting upon Him. And suddenly a voice came from heaven, saying, "This is My beloved Son, in whom I am well pleased."' (Matthew 3:13-17)

Jesus was aware of the Spirit's role and empowerment in His life, and this provided Him with a vision of what He would become. Jesus begins to picture walking and carrying out His Father's business.

"The human spirit fails, except when the Holy Spirit fills."
-Corrie Ten Boom

Once you become in tune to your help and resources, it serves as an assurance that you are not alone. Even Jesus knew He needed His Father and the Holy Spirit's assistance. He humbled and submitted Himself so that the power of God could flow through Him as a conduit.

4. Jesus' Purpose is Pursued.

Jesus selected 12 disciples, and they went on a Holy Ghost filled evangelistic crusade — healing the sick, feeding the hungry and sharing the gospel.

As powerful as Jesus is and was while on earth, He was still not a one-man show. He did many miracles, but still chose to create an alliance — a team He would disciple and send into ministry. Your purpose has to be initiated by you, but seldom is your purpose carried out solely by you. Those who have the greatest impact have surrounded themselves with like-minded individuals to assist in carrying out the vision God has planted within them. In fact, enlisting others causes the gift within to be expedited with speed. The individual who has the courage to start what God has put within them soon learns that it takes on a shape bigger and better than they envisioned.

5. Jesus' Purpose is Blocked.
Jesus was betrayed by someone in His own camp. Judas set Jesus up to be our Savior. Often we look at Judas as setting Jesus up for failure. In the physical realm, Judas' betrayal appeared to be a block to the success of Jesus' ministry. However, it would prove to be the passageway for the greatest gift to mankind — the perfect sacrifice to redeem the soul of man.

This stage of Jesus' purpose was a time of great distress, so much so, that He wept in the Garden of Gethsemane and prayed, "Father, if it is Your will, take this cup away from Me..." (Luke 22:42) No one is thrilled with the idea of pain and death. Yet, to be a savior, one must be willing to die. Every seed that produces more fruit, has to first die. It is the law of reproduction.

6. Jesus' Purpose is Put on Hold.
After Jesus' death, He spent three days in the tomb. He was put in a holding pattern, unable to move and only able to rest. Resolve in your mind to imitate Jesus and rest when you are in your place of holding. Don't resist, push or pull — simply rest. Even though you may walk through the valley of the shadow of death, know that God is with you. You must realize it is just a shadow. It is only an appearance or illusion while

you are going through it. As I have stated before, "Adversity is the gatekeeper to success." That is why few experience it— because few are willing to go down the path that appears to be deathly; however, it is really the path to life.

7. Jesus' Purpose is Resurrected.

Jesus was resurrected, and His purpose was fulfilled as He closed the gap between God and mankind.

"But the gift is not like the trespass. For if the many died by the trespass of the one man, how much more did God's grace and the gift that came by the grace of the one man, Jesus Christ, overflow to the many! Nor can the gift of God be compared with the result of one man's sin: The judgment followed one sin and brought condemnation, but the gift followed many trespasses and brought justification." (Romans 5:15-16)

8. Jesus' Purpose is Experienced.

"So then, after the Lord had spoken to them, He was received up into heaven, and sat down at the right hand of God. And they went out and preached everywhere, the Lord working with them and confirming the word through the accompanying signs. Amen." (Mark 16:19-20)

Jesus purpose was fulfilled. The manger boy had completed the journey to Majestic King. Our Savior depicts the twofold benefits of deciding to live out the purpose God has put within you by faith.

1. Exaltation

Those who have the faith and courage to walk out the riches within will be rewarded for their faithfulness. I believe that this reward will not only be experienced in Heaven, but here on earth. The principal of increase and abundance is directly proportional to giving. It is the Law of Production. It has to work because it is based on the Word of God.

"...what a man sows that will he also reap."(Galatians 6:7)

2. Expansion

"God is as committed to you as He is to Jesus; and will do for you what He did for Jesus."
-Joe Boatwright

The second benefit to living out your purpose is that what you start will increase. Your purpose will expand beyond your wildest imagination. Just as Jesus multiplied the two loaves and fishes, so He will cause your seed to expand. That is the nature of a seed. When it is planted, it sprouts and the cycle of reproduction just continues. Always remember, you may never truly know just how powerful that seed you sow will grow.

Walt Disney's Cycle
from a Nobody to Notorious

"What can become of a person
can not be detected in the infant or seed state."
-Guy E. Earle

Let's look at a modern example of someone who experienced the dream cycle. Walt Disney is a household name, but not everyone knows how his dream unfolded. In this chapter, I will share with you how Walt encountered the dream cycle adapting key details of his story from the book, *Walt Disney Conversations*, by Kathy Merlock Jackson.

1. Walt Disney's Purpose is Predestined.

Walt Disney believed that the world needed laughter. Who knew that on December 5, 1901, God would plant the seed of joy and laughter within him. In spite of the many obstacles he faced, Disney would unleash the gift of laughter through cartoon and entertainment to the world.

2. Walt Disney's Purpose is Aroused.

When Walt Disney was just a boy, he and his family moved to Missouri hoping for a more wholesome country life. Young Walt developed an interest in drawing and nature.

3. Purpose is Envisioned

Walt Disney was a man of great imagination. Along with

laughter, imagination is one of the greatest gifts he has given to the world—the ability to imagine what can be. His life is a great example of how purpose grows bigger than what we could ever envision. The seed of one man has produced Walt Disney Studios, which includes Walt Disney pictures, Touchstone Pictures, Walt Disney Studios Home Entertainment, Disney Theatrical Productions, Disney Live Family Entertainment and Disney on Ice—not to mention Disney Records and Hollywood Records. Disney's parks and resorts include Disney Cruise Line, Disneyland Resort—California, Disney World—Florida, Tokyo Disney Resort, Disneyland Resort—Paris, and Hong Kong Disneyland. Disney Media Networks include the Disney ABC Television Group and Radio Disney Network. All this from the seed of one man's purpose. Ponder just how big your purpose might grow, if you envisioned the seed on the inside of you.

> "Disneyland will never be completed. It will continue to grow as long as there is imagination left in the world.
> -Walt Disney

4. Walt Disney's Purpose Pursued.

In 1915 at age 14, Walt Disney took his first professional art lessons at the Kansas City Art Institute. In 1918, Walt Disney joined the Red Cross Ambulance Corps as a driver and served in France during World War I. When he returned from the war, he worked as an apprentice for Pesmen-Rubin Commercial Artists. Shortly after, Disney got a job making animated cartoons for the Kansas City Slide Company. He enlisted the help of many friends and worked on a production they called, *Little Red Riding Hood.* He resigned at twenty-one and formed a corporation which produced modernized children stories.

Walt was doing well. He bought a used movie camera, married Miss Bounds and hired an old artist friend from Kansas to work as his partner. His team also included 20 other artists he personally trained. He was hired by a New York buyer to create a cartoon film and had even bought a very nice automobile. He was living the life. Then, out of nowhere he heard a rumor that the buyer for his film was making other arrangements, and 20 of the artists he had personally trained, along with his partner, were planning on bailing on him. Refusing to believe it, he and his bride took a belated honeymoon to New York. The rumors proved true. All his dreams appeared to be in jeopardy.

5. Walt Disney's Purpose Blocked.
Walt experienced a major setback and fell $15,000 in debt. Walt and his bride decided to relocate to Hollywood and booked a train ride from New York to California. Walt was so upset that Mrs. Disney said, 'He was like a raging lion. The hurt, the pain the disappointment, the loss of trust was very evident…He kept saying, "I will never work for anyone else, I will be my own boss."' It was on the train ride from New York to California, however, that adversity presented an equal opportunity to advance him.

"All the adversity I've had in my life, all my troubles and obstacles, have strengthened me… You may not realize it when it happens, but a kick in the teeth may be the best thing in the world for you."
-Walt Disney

To release that negative energy, Walt begin to doodle on the railroad stationary and created a new cartoon idea call Plane Crazy. (Lindbergh had just astonished the world with his airplane flight). The star of the cartoon creation was a mouse, and he called it Mortimer. He read the script to Mrs. Disney, and the only thing she could respond to was the horrible name of the mouse, "Mortimer." A while later Walt asked her, "What do you think of the name, Mickey — Mickey Mouse?" She responded, "It sounds better than Mortimer!" And that is how Mickey Mouse was born.

6. Walt Disney's Purpose Put on Hold

There was a long spell before Disney's idea of Mickey would take off. His purpose appeared to be put on hold. During this season, Walt suffered a nervous breakdown due to exhaustion from overwork, and he had to rest to restore himself.

7. Walt Disney's Purpose is Resurrected.

In the same year of his breakdown, Mickey Mouse became a worldwide phenomenon, and the Mickey Mouse Club reached a million members — during the great Depression mind you. He went on to create numerous cartoon characters and short and long films including *The Three Little Pigs*, in 1933, *Donald Duck* in 1934, *Dumbo* in 1941, *Bambi* in 1942, *Cinderella* in 1950, *Alice in Wonderland* in 1951, *Robin Hood* in 1952, *Davey Crocket* in 1955, *Sleeping Beauty* and *The Shaggy Dog* in 1959 and *A Hundred and One Dalmatians* and *The Parent Trap* in 1961. It is interesting that most of Walt Disney's creations were birthed early on through an idea but didn't come into existence until a later time.

8. Walt Disney's Harvest is Experienced.

Walt Disney reaped a harvest and his harvest continues to grow. The vision to produce happiness and laughter was not only experienced, it was surpassed. Even during the Great Depression, Walt Disney provided a relief from all the pain that many experienced in the U.S. through laughter and family entertainment. His gift keeps on giving to this very day.

From entertainment parks to movies, television shows and music, the Disney empire goes on and on. Clearly he has produced much fruit, and I believe God said to him, "Well done thy good and faithful servant."

What You Sow on Purpose
Will Grow on Purpose

*"The law of harvest is to reap more than you sow. Sow an act,
and you reap a habit. Sow a habit, and you reap a character.
Sow a character, and you reap a destiny."*
-James Allen

T he biblical equation for all success is to plant, cultivate and reap a harvest. The Bible says, "there is seed time and harvest time." (Genesis 8:22) Clearly there is a progression, and then there is provision. The progression: you must plant; it must take root; it begins to bud; and eventually it comes full cycle and blooms (also called harvest).

The provision is that the harvest is made available beyond just the one who plants and sows. A harvest produces more with the purpose of being given and shared. Jesus, when he multiplied the two fish and five loaves, did it to share with others. Our lives are not to be a cul-de-sac but a conduit.

Life is not about hoarding what you have, it is about giving away what you have to make a difference. The Bible doesn't say that seedtime and harvest time are at the same time. However, that is often what we, as impatient human beings, desire. There cannot be a harvest without there being a season of sowing first.

It is vital that you grasp the principle of productivity, because you may be reaping for a season, but that season will end. The only guarantee of continued reaping is if there is continued sowing. One cannot rest on yesterday's sowing, or you may find yourself repeating the words of Solomon in Proverbs 6:6-11:

"Go to the ant, you sluggard;
* consider its ways and be wise!*
It has no commander,
* no overseer or ruler,*
yet it stores its provisions in summer
* and gathers its food at harvest.*
How long will you lie there, you sluggard?
* When will you get up from your sleep?*
A little sleep, a little slumber,
* a little folding of the hands to rest —*
and poverty will come on you like a thief
* and scarcity like an armed man."*

What I want to impress upon you is that you can bring to harvest the seeds of greatness God has placed within you at birth. You sow your seed of greatness by first becoming aware of it and deeply appreciating it.

"Satan is the number one headhunter in the world. He has the ability to see your greatness before it springs forth into reality. Therefore, he wants to keep us unaware of our seed and its potential."
-Guy E. Earle

I once told someone, who had the gift of decorating, that once they valued and cherished their gift as much as others did, their gift would multiply and produce. Often we don't recognize the seed as great, because it is in the seed form. However, Satan is the number one headhunter in the world. He has the ability to see your greatness before it springs forth into reality. Therefore, he wants to keep us unaware of our seed and its potential. God has blessed you with seeds of greatness, so you can be a blessing!

"I am the true vine, and my Father is the gardener. He cuts off every branch in me that bears no fruit, while every branch that does bear fruit he prunes so that it will be even more fruitful. You are already clean because of the word I have spoken to you. Remain in me, as I also remain in you. No branch can bear fruit by itself; it must remain in the vine. Neither can you bear fruit unless you remain in me. I am the vine; you are the branches. If you remain in me and I in you, you will bear much fruit; apart from me you can do nothing. If you do not remain in me, you are like a branch that is thrown away and withers; such branches are picked up, thrown into the fire and burned. If you remain in me and my words remain in you, ask whatever you wish, and it will be done for you. This is to my Father's glory, that you bear much fruit, showing yourselves to be my disciples." (John 15:1-8)

God's intention for your seed is that it would bear much fruit. If you know anything about fruit, you know it spoils fast. It is of no use or value simply to hoard fruit gathered. Your fruit is meant to be given away. As you give it away, it will continue to grow.

"You cannot hold on to anything good. You must be continually giving and getting. You cannot hold on to your seed. You must sow it and reap anew. You cannot hold on to riches. You must use them and get other riches in return."
-Robert Collier

What happens when a seed is planted in the ground? With the right combination of sun, soil and water, the seed undergoes a process of growth to reach maturity. The steps between seed form and becoming a full plant don't

happen overnight. It takes patience, a process and persever-
ance for the plant to grow to its full potential. It starts off small
but has the potential to grow big; it just takes time. The life
cycle of a seed progresses like this:

1. Seed planted
2. Seed cultivated and develops a root
3. Root produces budding
4. Root births a small plant
5. Small plant matures

Notice how the cycle of a plant looks a lot like the cycle of a
purpose fulfilled. Seeds start off insignificant, but they have
an exponential capacity for multiplication. If you plant a seed

in the ground, it sprouts and a new plant grows producing new seeds. The plant's life cycle can then repeat an infinite number of times. However, if the first seed is never planted, nothing will happen. God has designed it that our gift can have an immeasurable impact as well, but it all starts with you. If you never take that which God has put within in and sow it, it doesn't have the capability to reproduce. In fact, God is expecting you to multiply the gifts and talents he has given you.

"Again, it will be like a man going on a journey, who called his servants and entrusted his wealth to them. To one he gave five bags of gold, to another two bags, and to another one bag, each according to his ability. Then he went on his journey. The man who had received five bags of gold went at once and put his money to work and gained five bags more. So also, the one with two bags of gold gained two more. But the man who had received one bag went off, dug a hole in the ground and hid his master's money.

After a long time the master of those servants returned and settled accounts with them. The man who had received five bags of gold brought the other five. 'Master,' he said, 'you entrusted me with five bags of gold. See, I have gained five more.'

His master replied, 'Well done, good and faithful servant! You have been faithful with a few things; I will put you in charge of many things. Come and share your master's happiness!'

The man with two bags of gold also came. 'Master,' he said, 'you entrusted me with two bags of gold; see, I have gained two more.'

His master replied, 'Well done, good and faithful servant! You have been faithful with a few things; I will put you in charge of many things. Come and share your master's happiness!'

Then the man who had received one bag of gold came. 'Master,' he said, 'I knew that you are a hard man, harvesting where you have not sown and gathering where you have not scattered seed. So I was afraid and went out and hid your gold in the ground. See, here is what belongs to you.'

His master replied, 'You wicked, lazy servant! So you knew that I harvest where I have not sown and gather where I have not scattered seed? Well then, you should have put my money on deposit with the bankers, so that when I returned I would have received it back with interest. So take the bag of gold from him and give it to the one who has ten bags. For whoever has will be given more, and they will have an abundance. Whoever does not have, even what they have will be taken from them. And throw that worthless servant outside, into the darkness, where there will be weeping and gnashing of teeth.' "
(Matthew 25:14-28)

In a nutshell: if you don't use the gift you have been given, you will lose it. You have a divine opportunity to duplicate the character of Jesus by giving of yourself. Yet, there is only a small window to maximize your time in this realm. Don't be like the unfaithful servant with your talent and seed and hide it away and do nothing with it out of fear. Regardless of how big or small your talent is, embrace it; envision what can be and engage in actions that will yield a harvest.

Putting the Cycle of a
Purpose Fulfilled into Action

"A real decision is measured by the fact that you've taken a
new action. If there's no action, you haven't truly decided."
-Tony Robbins

At the end of the day, all the seeds of greatness God has put in you won't amount to anything, if you never take any action to plant, grow and develop them. Your action is critical to your purpose fulfillment. It does no good to read these pages and learn the principles if you are not prepared to take action. But, I believe you are a person of action, otherwise you wouldn't be holding this book in your hands now. In fact, I believe you picked up this book at the perfect time and God has been grooming you for greatness. The cycle of a purpose fulfilled is ready to begin in your life, or if it has already begun, then it's time to take it to the next level. Its time to walk it out step-by-step.

I love this chapter, because I get to share with you some practical, everyday steps that you can put into action in your life. Take your time as you go through these exercises and meditate on your responses. You may want to work through these exercises in a day or over the course of a week or several weeks. The important thing is that you complete all of these exercises and begin to implement them in your day-to-day life.

As you begin to take action, you are going to see your purpose unfold little by little. Remember, it's a process, not a one-stop destination. I believe in you, but what's more...God believes in you! Ready, set, action!

Stage 1: Your Purpose is Predestined.

Ask God to help you to clearly be able to express what your divine purpose and calling is.

A. God called Moses to deliver the great nation of Israel out of Egypt.
B. God called David to become a mighty king.
C. God called Jesus to be the Savior for all mankind.
D. God called Walt Disney to share the gift of laughter through art and nature.

Finish this sentence. God has called me to _____

_____

_____

_____

_____

What if I don't know? Oftentimes your calling—that seed within you that desires to give birth—is in the form of:

1. Passion—What do you have a burning desire for? What are you passionate to see happen in life? One person may desire justice and make it the driving force of their life. They may want to see truth and justice prevail over evil. This passion may lead them to be a judge, police officer, probation office or even the President of the United States.

Describe what your burning passion is. It could be in just one area or many. _____

_____

_____

_____

_____

2. Perturb — What frustrates or troubles you greatly? One person may get disturbed when they see poverty. This motivation may inspire them to teach people how to prosper or become an entrepreneur, social worker, philanthropist, or even an activist to inspire social change. Create a list of the things that perturb you.

_____

_____

_____

_____

3. Pen — Create a Mission Statement. Put in writing your purpose and intent for life.

Tips on Developing a MISSION Statement

I have created the acronym M.I.S.S.I.O.N to highlight the key aspects of your mission and to aid you in putting on paper the wealth of resources you possess and how you desire to disseminate them. A mission statement can also be called a passion statement.

M-Motivate — What motivates you to take action?

What is it that causes you to loose track of time — to overlook the fact that you haven't eaten in eight hours because you are so engaged? What is that thing that inspires noble feelings within you? Describe your motivation._____

_____

_____

_____

_____

I-Irritate — What irritates you in life?

What is it that causes you to cringe — that causes you to say, "enough is enough...I need to do something about this?" List your causes and irritations._____

_____

_____

_____

_____

S-Success — What past or present successes have you experienced?

What have you accomplished that brought about a sense of great gratitude? What good deeds have you done that taught you it is more blessed to give than to receive? List your successes._____

_____

_____

_____

_____

S-Share — What do you posses*in the form of resources, knowledge, craft, talent or ability, that you can give away? List them.

_____

_____

_____

_____

I-Identify core values — What is your inner compass pointing you towards? What are the core values and attributes that fuel you? (i.e. integrity, truth, justice, etc.). Spell out your core values.

_____

_____

_____

_____

O-Objectives — What objectives, ideas and goals do you what want to accomplish?

Don't allow your goals to be defined by what you see now, the lack of money or resources or how difficult your goals may be. Write out your ideas, goals and objectives below as if anything was possible — because it is!_____

_____

_____

_____

_____

N-Notebook — Purchase a notebook or journal in which you can write down, in a simple statement, a summary of what the riches and resources God has placed within you will look like when unleashed. Use this notebook or journal to process and spell out how you will accomplish your mission. Just begin writing, and before you know it, you will awaken the riches within. You will be ready to begin the cycle of a purpose fulfilled.

For now, on the lines provided here, write your summary statement of the riches and resources you possess._____

_____

_____

_____

_____

4. Ponder—Become grateful for the gift God has put within you at birth. Take time to ponder quietly and appreciate what God has put within you. Ask God to help you cherish your gifts and receive His guidance on how to develop your seeds of greatness into mature fruit.

"When you stop taking your gift for granted and truly appreciate it and honor it, your gift will grant you enormous success and opportunity."
-Guy E. Earle

Stage 2: Your Purpose is Aroused.

This step is a continuation from Stage 1 — Purpose Predestined. I want you to continue to explore what God put within you.

1. Take personal inventory of your assets, abilities and experiences by answering the following questions.

THE CYCLE OF A PURPOSE FULFILLED

a. What would I do for free?_____

_____

_____

_____

_____

b. What do others say I am good at?_____

_____

_____

_____

_____

c. What is my unfair advantage? Identify what it is that you do naturally and with ease while others have to struggle at it. I had a client come into my office, and I was helping him get back on track with his purpose. His love for numbers came up. He was able to calculate any number I gave him by 25. As I tested him, he rattled off each number like he was reading it off of a cheat sheet. I was very impressed and he said, "Oh it is super easy; let me show you how to do it." Let me tell you I will be using my calculator, for it didn't seem all that easy to me when he showed me how he did it. This was his unfair advantage and was a clue to what he was created for. What is your unfair advantage? Write it down._____

_____

_____

_____

_____

2. Take a personal assessment inventory. I personally like the RAISEC inventory because it breaks down who you are into the following six categories:

1. Realistic
2. Investigative
3. Artistic
4. Social
5. Enterprising
6. Conventional

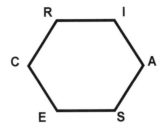

The RAISEC was created by John L. Holland. He observed that there are six areas (RAISEC) that describe individuals as it relates to career choices. He suggests that each person gravitates to one or two areas in particular. It is helpful to know those in selecting meaningful work. Here is a brief description of the six areas. If you are struggling to find a suitable occupation or just want to know more about your personal bent, I recommend that you use this great assessment tool.

√**Realistic**—This person is attracted to outdoor, mechanical and physical activity. They prefer working with things, objects and animals rather than with data, ideas and people.

Investigative—This person is naturally curious and inquisitive. They have a need to understand, explain and predict the things that go on around them.

Artistic—This person is creative, original and individualistic. They like to be different and stand out from the crowd.

√**Social**—These people are friendly and outgoing. They are cooperative and enjoy working with and being around other people. They posses the ability to understand others' feelings and problems. They are often in service roles.

Enterprising—This person is self-confident, outgoing and optimistic. They like to organize, direct and control the activities of the group. They are in the business of influencing the opinions and actions of others.

Conventional — This person is well-organized, persistent and practical in their approach to life. They enjoy working with numbers, records or machines in a set, orderly way. They generally avoid ambiguous unstructured activities.

Stage 3: Your Purpose is Envisioned.

"God, who gives life to the dead and calls those things which do not exist as though they did." (Romans 4:17)

God calls things into existence that are not, as if they already were. Creation is an account of God calling into existence something that had no existence. In Romans 4, Abraham's faith affords him the ability to envision what looked impossible and see it as reality — a son from his seed and Sarah's womb.

"Man sees his failure or success, his joy or sorrow, before it swings into visibility from scenes set in his own imagination."
–Florence Scovel Shinn

"Faith is the substance of things hoped for, and the evidence of things not seen." (Hebrews 11:1)

Your faith has nothing to do with what you see physically, but your faith has everything to do with what you see mentally.

What will your vision and purpose look like in real life? Write it down; picture it like a movie. When God gave a promise in scripture, He sometimes provided a picture to depict what the promise would look like. He told Abram, "I will make you the Father of a great nation." (Genesis 12:2, 17:5) He gave him the picture of the stars in Heaven to depict how great and large that nation would be. (Genesis 14:5)

1. Take some time to journal, with all the vivid details and senses you can arise, what your purpose will look like when it arrives. Get yourself in a state "as if" what it is you see is already done. If you can believe, all things are possible!

Stage 4: Your Purpose is Pursued.

This is a time of action. As you begin to focus your time and mind on unleashing the gift God has placed within you, you will begin to get ideas. Ideas and hunches are often not acted upon, but that is a great mistake. Once you get the idea, move at once. One idea can set you free financially. Every great accomplishment started with an idea or a hunch that was acted upon.

1. Sit daily in mediation asking God for divine direction on how you can most effectively carry out the mission He has for you.

2. Examine what resources and people are presently in your life who can aid you in the process of obtaining your goal.

3. Nike's motto is "Just do it." This simple phrase is about getting into action. Don't worry about perfection or obstacles. Just take what you have and begin to move forward in faith. God will either remove the obstacle or use the obstacle to direct your steps to a place you most likely would have never arrived had it not been for the obstacle.

In my book, *Transformed Through His Thoughts*, I introduce the Ultimate Success Formula:

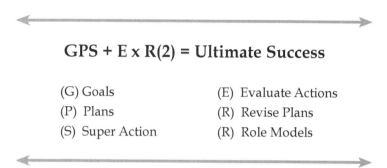

GPS + E x R(2) = Ultimate Success

(G) Goals	(E) Evaluate Actions
(P) Plans	(R) Revise Plans
(S) Super Action	(R) Role Models

In this formula is Super Action. Action is nothing more than faith with feet. In the Bible, Nehemiah and the builders were able to accomplish their goals in record time, because they accelerated their action.

"In all hard work there is a profit, but merely talking about it only brings poverty." (Proverbs 14:2)

Stage 5: Your Purpose is Blocked.

"For the vision is yet for an appointed time;
But at the end it will speak, and it will not lie.
Though it tarries, wait for it;
Because it will surely come,
It will not tarry." (Habakkuk 2:3)

You must hold in your heart that what God has put in it will be accomplished, if you do your part. Yes, you have a responsibility. Like the parable of the faithful servant versus the unfaithful servant, the only difference between the two was their action or what I call "faith." But what happens when your actions are blocked and when your efforts appear to be futile? This is the time to affirm to yourself.

"Though it tarries, wait for it; because it will surely come." (Habakkuk 2:3)

When you get to this place of being blocked, keep moving but evaluate your actions. Perhaps you are just spinning your wheels. Slow down and take personal inventory. This season is often bumpy and unpleasant so allow yourself to be refreshed by putting your trust in God and not your actions.

1. Learn the art of being still. Reflect on the verse, "Be still and know that I am God."(Psalms 46:10)

a. Ask God, "What is it that I need to do or not do in this phase?"

b. Ask yourself, "What areas in my life do I need to adjust so that I am aligned perfectly with God and His purpose?"

"Faith goes up the stairs that love has built and looks out the window which hope has opened."
-- Charles Spurgeon

2. Learn the art of praising God in the dark.

a. Thank God for His ability to accomplish what He said He would regardless of whether you see how or not. Learn to praise him before you see how He will work things out.

"Being confident of this very thing, that He who has begun a good work in you will complete it until the day of Jesus Christ." (Philippians 1:6)

Stage 6: Your Purpose is Put on Hold.

Similar to your purpose being blocked, when you are in a holding pattern, it isn't that you are not going to reach your destination. It's just that you are not going to reach your destination on your timetable. Often when an airplane is in a holding pattern, it is already very close to the destination. Yet, the destination is not ready for the plane. Perhaps you are already ready, but what God is preparing for you is not or vise versa. Nevertheless, wait on the Lord.

"But those who wait on the LORD
   Shall renew their strength;
   They shall mount up with wings like eagles,
   They shall run and not be weary,
   They shall walk and not faint." (Isaiah 40:31)

1. Restore your soul. Before a big event, which will require much exertion, it is wise to get rest prior to. View this holding pattern as an opportunity to refuel, refresh and refocus. You will be in the battle quick enough.

a. What can you do to refuel and refresh yourself during this waiting period? Write it down.

_____

_____

_____

_____

Stage 7: Your Purpose is Resurrected.

It is game time. It is time to get back into action! Answer these questions.

1. What did God show me in my waiting period?

_____

_____

_____

_____

2. Now go and implement what God showed you. Don't sec-ond-guess it; don't doubt it. Just do it!

3. What things are in you (character weaknesses, bad habits, challenge spots, etc.) that can hinder your success? Whether it is anger, fear, an inability to manage your money or an ad-diction, your weak areas will show up and ruin the party. It is important to fully grasp that it is easier to get to your destina-tion than it is to maintain your success. If you can pinpoint your weak areas, you can work on correcting them now, so they won't be a hindrance to your success in the future._____

_____

_____

_____

_____

Stage 8: Your Harvest Time is Experienced.

This is a time of reaping and harvest. Congratulations, you have arrived. Take a deep breath and enjoy and give thanks for the blessings you are partaking off. Celebrate your suc-cess and the wonderful ways God has shown His faithfulness throughout the process.

As you take time to enjoy your purpose fulfilled, know that it not a one-time or one-stop destination. Your purpose cycle will repeat and last your whole life long. God's intention for your seed is that it bear much fruit and continue to bear fruit. Realize that your reaping is experienced because of your previous sowing. Don't get so caught up in partaking of the fruit of your yesterday that you fail to sow today. Take time to ponder this question and write down your insights.

What seeds can you begin to sow today?_____

_____

_____

_____

_____

Then, get started sowing again. I promise, if you continue to follow God's purpose cycle for your life, you will go from faith to faith and victory to victory and bless the lives of countless others. Continue to sow and grow and watch God take you where you never thought you could go!

ABOUT THE AUTHOR

Guy E. Earle is an inspirational speaker, professional counselor, certified wellness coach, and certified practitioner in the area of trauma therapy. Presently he serves as the Director of Counseling for Oak Cliff Bible Fellowship in Dallas, Texas—an 8,000 member congregation—where Dr. Tony Evans is the Senior Pastor. Guy earned a Masters degree in Theology and Pastoral Counseling from Dallas Theological Seminary and a Masters in Marriage and Family Counseling from Southwestern Baptist Theological Seminary.

For more information or to contact Guy, visit:
www.guyeearle.com.

OTHER WORKS BY GUY E. EARLE

Transformed Through His Thoughts: Achieve Change by Replacing Destructive Thoughts with God's Thoughts (BOOK)

Free from Destructive Thoughts (DVD)

The Power of Faith (DVD)

The Power of Forgiveness (DVD)

To order these products or to
book Guy E. Earle to speak at your next event, visit:
www.guyeearle.com.

Made in the USA
Charleston, SC
07 May 2012